Original title:
The Essence of Empathy

Copyright © 2024 Swan Charm
All rights reserved.

Author: Olivia Orav
ISBN HARDBACK: 978-9916-86-908-6
ISBN PAPERBACK: 978-9916-86-909-3
ISBN EBOOK: 978-9916-86-910-9

The Depths of Shared Experience

In the hush of twilight's glow,
Whispers weave a tale of old,
Hands entwined, hearts aglow,
Stories shared, treasures told.

Waves of laughter, soft and clear,
Echo through the night's embrace,
In your gaze, I hold you near,
Finding home in every space.

Through the trials, thick and thin,
We navigate the wild seas,
With each loss, we find a win,
In our bond, we find keys.

Moments pass, yet we remain,
Rooted deep as ancient trees,
Bearing joy, enduring pain,
Together, dancing with the breeze.

In the silence, dreams take flight,
A tapestry of souls as one,
In this depth, we find our light,
A journey shared, never done.

When Hearts Align

In quiet corners, love starts to glow,
Two souls entwined, a dance so slow.
Whispers of fate in a gentle breeze,
Moments like this bring the heart to ease.

Under the stars, we share our dreams,
Filling the silence with hopeful beams.
Every glance a promise, every touch a sign,
In the still of the night, when hearts align.

Reflections of Another

In mirrors we find what we wish to see,
Shadows of others as part of me.
Each story shared is a thread in the weave,
Understanding grows when we dare to believe.

Through whispered tales of laughter and tears,
We bridge the gaps of our hopes and fears.
In every heartbeat echoes a tone,
Reflections of another, we are never alone.

Beneath the Surface

The ocean deep holds secrets untold,
Currents that shift, both gentle and bold.
What lies beneath may never be clear,
Yet beauty abounds, drawing us near.

A world unexplored with treasures to find,
In depths of the heart, where love is blind.
Dive into layers, let go of control,
Beneath the surface, we uncover the soul.

The Language of Listening

In silence, we hear what words cannot say,
Emotions conveyed in their own special way.
A nod and a smile, the heart's subtle plea,
The language of listening sets our spirits free.

With patience, we gather the stories unseen,
In moments of stillness, the spaces between.
Connection unfolds without need for a sound,
In the language of listening, true love is found.

Shared Breath of Existence

In the quiet of dawn's embrace,
Whispers entwine, a gentle grace.
Each heartbeat sings, a soft refrain,
Life's thread connects, joy and pain.

In the rustling leaves, tales unfold,
Stories of warmth, both young and old.
Nature's canvas, painted bright,
Every breath shared, ignites the light.

Mirrors of Experience

Reflections dance in twilight's glow,
Memories flicker, ebb and flow.
Through laughter's tears, truths are found,
In every echo, love is crowned.

The paths we walk, both rough and kind,
Shape the hearts, forever entwined.
Mirrors show the love we seek,
In every glance, connection speaks.

Sails of Sympathy

Across the sea, our feelings drift,
With every wave, a gentle gift.
Sails of hope carry us high,
Together we journey, you and I.

In storms we find, the strength to steer,
Holding close those we hold dear.
Kindred spirits, side by side,
In the heart's ocean, we abide.

Heartstrings Entwined

In the still of a warm embrace,
Feel the pulse of a sacred place.
Threads of love, woven tight,
In shadows and sun, we find our light.

With every moment, stories grow,
In silent whispers, hearts bestow.
Entwined like vines in a dance,
Together we weave our sweetest chance.

Kindred Spirits Collide

In twilight's glow, we find our place,
Two souls aligned in gentle grace.
The spark ignites, a dance begins,
Together forever, through thick and thin.

With laughter shared, and dreams we forge,
In whispered secrets, love will surge.
A bond so strong, it breaks all chains,
In kindred hearts, no room for pains.

Through storms and trials, hand in hand,
In every heartbeat, we understand.
No greater joy than this embrace,
Our spirits soar, in time and space.

In every glance, a story told,
In every touch, a warmth to hold.
With every moment, time suspends,
As kindred spirits, the journey bends.

Rhythms of Togetherness

In the morning light, we rise as one,
With every heartbeat, our day's begun.
The world around us fades away,
As we dance to the rhythm of the day.

The softest whispers in the breeze,
Guide our path with effortless ease.
In laughter's echo, joy resounds,
In every step, true love abounds.

Through ups and downs, we sway and bend,
In melodies that never end.
With hands entwined, we stroll the way,
In the harmony of what we play.

In twilight's hue, we find our song,
In the warmth of love, we both belong.
Together still, through night's embrace,
We find our rhythm, our sacred space.

A Glimpse Through Another's Eyes

In silence deep, we share the light,
A window open, a shared insight.
Through whispered dreams, we see anew,
A glimpse of life, through what you view.

In painted hues, the world unfolds,
A story rich, in layers told.
With every breath, we journey near,
In your eyes, I find no fear.

The laughter bright, the teardrops fall,
In every moment, we feel it all.
Through your heart, I sense the sky,
A deeper love that won't run dry.

In shadows cast, and light that shines,
We find the threads that intertwine.
A tapestry of souls combined,
Through every glimpse, our hearts aligned.

Heartstrings Unraveled

In quiet corners, secrets lie,
With heartstrings pulled, they softly sigh.
Each tale we're weaving, thread by thread,
With every heartbeat, love is spread.

Through tangled paths, we learn and grow,
In gentle whispers, feelings flow.
With every touch, a story starts,
As heartstrings dance, we join our hearts.

The chords of life, they twist and bend,
In every moment, my love, my friend.
A symphony of dreams unfurled,
In your embrace, I find my world.

With laughter bright, and sorrows shared,
In every glance, we know we cared.
Together strong, we stand and fight,
With heartstrings unraveled, we find our light.

Tides of Compassion

In the quiet night, hearts flow,
Gentle whispers, kindness to show.
Each wave a promise, soft and true,
A world united, me and you.

Cycles of empathy, we share,
Brushing away burdens with care.
Tides of love rise, never cease,
In every challenge, find sweet peace.

Hands joined together, strong and bright,
We lift each other, spread the light.
Beneath the stars, our spirits soar,
Compassion's tide opens the door.

In moments tough, we find our way,
Guided by hope, come what may.
Embracing differences, we find grace,
In the embrace of love's warm face.

So let the currents flow in trust,
With open hearts, it's more than just.
Together we'll sail, forever free,
In the compassion among you and me.

Mirrors of the Soul

In reflections deep, we find our way,
Glimmers of truth in night and day.
Each gaze a story, quietly told,
Mirrors of the soul, bright and bold.

Flickers of laughter, shadows of pain,
Every smile carved by joy or rain.
In eyes like oceans, secrets lie,
Our inner worlds reach for the sky.

In silence shared, we learn to see,
The beauty in you, the strength in me.
With every glance, a bridge we build,
In the depths of hearts, love fulfilled.

From cracks and flaws, we rise anew,
Reflections of grace in all we do.
Together we dance, under the sun,
Mirrors of the soul, forever one.

In the space between us, hope will bloom,
In the quiet corners, we find room.
To discover ourselves, and in each gaze,
Seeing the light in endless ways.

Embracing the Unseen

In the shadows, dreams take flight,
Whispers of courage in the night.
What's hidden deep, we learn to find,
Embracing the unseen, heart and mind.

Beneath the surface, wisdom flows,
In silent moments, true self grows.
The dance of hope lightly unfurls,
In the unseen depths of our worlds.

To trust the whispers, feel the call,
In stillness, rise above it all.
Through unseen bonds, we tie and weave,
In the unseen, we learn to believe.

A spark ignites in every heart,
In the quiet, we play our part.
Embrace the mystery, feel the grace,
In the unseen spaces, love finds its place.

With open arms, we take the leap,
Daring to dream, embracing hope steep.
In the silence, we will find our way,
Embracing the unseen, day by day.

Bridges Across Solitude

In the stillness, a voice calls near,
Calling to hearts, both far and clear.
Constructing bridges with threads of gold,
Connecting stories that need to be told.

With every step, a path revealed,
In shared silence, the soul is healed.
Across the void, we reach our hands,
Bridges of hope in distant lands.

Embracing whispers, truths we share,
In our togetherness, we find care.
Across the chasms, we'll build our dreams,
In love's embrace, nothing's as it seems.

So take the leap, let courage rise,
With every heartbeat, cut through the lies.
In moments bright, in shadows long,
Together we stand, silent yet strong.

For solitude welcomes the brave in soul,
A journey together makes the heart whole.
Across the bridges, let's walk side by side,
In the dance of life, we shall abide.

A Symphony of Hearts

In the silence, beats arise,
Together, they create the skies.
Harmonies of love entwined,
Echo through each heart inclined.

The notes of joy, a soft embrace,
In every rhythm, find their place.
Together we sing, side by side,
In this symphony, we confide.

Melodies weave a tale so sweet,
With every heartbeat, we repeat.
Dancing under the moonlight's glow,
A symphony only we know.

Each heart a story, rich and grand,
In perfect tune, hand in hand.
Together in sorrow, together in cheer,
A timeless song that we hold dear.

With every crescendo, emotions soar,
In harmony, we find our core.
A symphony of hearts so true,
Together, we create anew.

Unity in Diversity

Colors blend in a vivid dance,
Cultures rich, a true expanse.
Together we stand, hand in hand,
In this diversity, we understand.

Voices rise in melody bright,
A chorus of hope, a shining light.
Different paths, but one great goal,
Unity flows within the soul.

From every corner, stories unfold,
Tales of courage, journeys bold.
In laughter and joy, in struggles we face,
Together we find our rightful place.

Minds open wide, with hearts so free,
An endless bond, just you and me.
Through every challenge, we will endure,
In our togetherness, we are pure.

Diversity is our cherished wealth,
In unity, we discover ourselves.
Different yet kind, forever we stand,
United in spirit, a vibrant land.

The Canvas of Togetherness

With brushes dipped in shades of dreams,
We paint a world of vibrant streams.
Every stroke, a story to tell,
On this canvas, we weave so well.

Colors swirl in harmony bright,
A masterpiece of hearts in flight.
Together we form a stunning scene,
In love's embrace, we find the sheen.

Each hue a voice, each line a thread,
In this creation, nothing is dead.
From darkest nights to dawn's first glow,
Together we flourish, together we grow.

The canvas whispers secrets so dear,
In every layer, love draws near.
In collaboration, we find our way,
Creating beauty day by day.

A tapestry woven by hands and hearts,
In unity, the magic starts.
Together as artists, we paint our fate,
On the canvas where we celebrate.

Heartfelt Translations

Words unspoken, feelings shared,
In silent moments, love is bared.
Through every glance, a story flows,
In this connection, true love grows.

With every heartbeat, we translate,
The language of love, our fates create.
In soft whispers, in gentle sighs,
We find the truth behind the lies.

Across the distance, hearts align,
In every pulse, destinies entwine.
Speaking softly without a sound,
In this bond, our souls are found.

Through laughter's echo and tears that fall,
In every heartbeat, we heed the call.
Translations of love, cherished and rare,
In the depths of our souls, forever we'll share.

With every breath, our stories unite,
In heartfelt translations, day turns to night.
Together we write this tale of ours,
In a world of love, beneath the stars.

Luminescent Connections

In twilight's glow, we find our way,
Soft whispers meld in shades of gray.
Stars above, they dance and gleam,
Binding hearts in a shared dream.

Glowing paths that intertwine,
Every moment, yours and mine.
Through the dark, our spirits shine,
Infinite love, a gift divine.

In laughter bright, in silence deep,
Memories made, ours to keep.
With every heartbeat, life's embrace,
In every glance, a warm trace.

We sail through storms, we rise as one,
Connected under the same sun.
With every tear, with every smile,
Together, we journey every mile.

A Warm Embrace of Solace

In the quiet, a soft breath flows,
A gentle touch, where kindness grows.
Wrapped within a tender space,
Heartbeats sync in a warm embrace.

When shadows fall and dreams feel far,
Your presence shines, a guiding star.
With open arms, you hold me tight,
Turning darkness into light.

In moments still, where silence speaks,
We find our strength, though life feels weak.
With whispered words, we mend the seams,
In solace found, we shape our dreams.

Through stormy nights and sunny days,
We navigate in countless ways.
In love's cocoon, we rise and thrive,
Each heartbeat echoes, we are alive.

The Threads that Bind Us

In colors rich, our stories weave,
Tales of joy and hearts that grieve.
A tapestry of love so bright,
Threads entwined in day and night.

With whispers soft, the fabric flows,
Carrying warmth in every throes.
United now, through thick and thin,
Each thread a tale of where we've been.

In laughter loud and tears that fall,
We find our strength, we stand tall.
Every moment, a mark defined,
In the threads of life, we're intertwined.

Together we rise, together we stand,
Life's vibrant weave, hand in hand.
In every heartbeat, love's sweet tune,
Under the sun, beneath the moon.

Beneath Exteriors

Behind the smiles, a depth unseen,
Stories hidden, calm and keen.
In every glance, a world unfolds,
Mysteries kept, and secrets told.

Layers form like petals in bloom,
Hiding dreams beneath the gloom.
In silence shared, we find the key,
To unlock hearts, to set them free.

With open minds, we dare to see,
The beauty found in you and me.
A spark ignites, a flame so bright,
Illuminating the darkest night.

Beneath the surface, depth anew,
In every heartbeat, a love true.
United we stand, souls on fire,
In this journey, we'll never tire.

Bridges of Understanding

Across the river, we reach out,
Hands extended, silencing doubt.
Every story shared, a gentle bend,
In the fabric of what we defend.

Two worlds merging, hearts aligned,
In the space between, we find what's kind.
Through open dialogue, walls will fall,
Together, united, we stand tall.

With each step taken, trust will bloom,
Lighting corners, dispelling gloom.
A bridge built on empathy's art,
Connecting souls, a brand new start.

In differences, we see the light,
Transforming shadows into bright.
What once divided, now can unite,
Crafting futures, pure delight.

So let us walk this path so wide,
With open hearts, side by side.
For every bridge that's built with care,
Creates the hope that we can share.

Whispers in the Heart

In quiet moments, whispers sound,
Secrets hidden, deeply profound.
Gentle echoes, soft and clear,
Carrying love to those we hold dear.

Behind the silence, stories lie,
Words unspoken, dreams that fly.
In every heartbeat, a sacred song,
Reminding us where we belong.

A gaze exchanged, a silent plea,
In the stillness, souls can see.
With every flutter, feelings rise,
In tender whispers, love defies.

Through trials faced, we find our way,
In whispers shared, we choose to stay.
A bond formed in the quiet night,
Guiding us toward the light.

These whispers linger, softly spun,
A tapestry woven, two become one.
In every heartbeat, a promise made,
In love's embrace, we won't be swayed.

Threads of Connection

In the loom of life, we weave our fate,
Threads entwined, never too late.
Each color vibrant, every line strong,
Together we create a lasting song.

With every twist, a tale unfolds,
Emotions stitched through highs and folds.
These fibers bond us in joyful ways,
Guiding through the toughest days.

From one heart to another, we send,
Embracing love that has no end.
In laughter shared, in tears we shed,
Each thread a word, a life well led.

Gathered together, so close in time,
In unity's rhythm, we find a rhyme.
Through every storm, the fabric's tight,
Beneath the stars, we shine so bright.

And when we glance at what we've sewn,
In every thread, seeds of love are grown.
For in this tapestry, we are found,
In connection's dance, joy abounds.

Kaleidoscope of Souls

In every glance, a story told,
Fragments of life, vibrant and bold.
Colors blending, creating a view,
A kaleidoscope, ever anew.

Each soul a hue, unique, divine,
Together we form a stunning design.
Reflecting dreams, hopes intertwined,
In this mosaic, warmth we find.

Through laughter's ring and sorrow's tear,
In shared moments, we grow near.
A spectrum shining, hand in hand,
In unity's embrace, we firmly stand.

With every twist, perspectives change,
In the dance of life, we rearrange.
Each turn a revelation, bright and clear,
In this lens of love, we conquer fear.

So let us marvel at this sight,
A kaleidoscope glowing, pure delight.
For in every soul's glow, we see,
The beauty in our diversity.

The Weight of a Whisper

In the hush of night, it lingers,
Carrying secrets, soft yet profound.
Gentle echoes weave through the dark,
A truth unspoken, deeply found.

Shadows dance beneath the moon's glow,
Each heartbeat stirs the stillness near.
With a breath, a world ignites,
In silence, hearts learn to hear.

The fragile threads of quiet trust,
Bind lives together, unseen but strong.
A whisper can bridge the vast divide,
Turning solitude into a song.

In the pauses, the warmth is shared,
A knowing glance, a moment's grace.
Through every sigh, we come alive,
In whispers, we discover our place.

So listen close, for words can hide,
In the weight of whispers, love abounds.
In the silences, we find our way,
Where the lost are finally found.

Pulse of Understanding

In the rhythm of hearts, we find sync,
A dance of thoughts, a seamless flow.
Each beat a promise, a tender link,
In silence, the truest feelings grow.

Eyes connect, no need for words,
In that moment, we truly see.
The pulse that thrums is felt in nerves,
A shared heartbeat, you and me.

Through storms we've walked, unmasked our fears,
Resilience blooms in shadowed ground.
With every tear, hope reappears,
In this pulse, our strength is found.

Listen closely to the silent sound,
In understanding, we bridge the gaps.
Where minds converge and souls confound,
In harmony, we close the maps.

Together, we rise through life's vast dance,
Each whisper shared, not lost, but held.
For in the pulse, there's a deep romance,
A bond unbroken, a love compelled.

Flickers of Connection

In quiet rooms where shadows play,
A glance ignites a spark anew.
Small gestures light the darkest way,
Flickers of hope in shades of blue.

Hands brush gently in the night,
Carrying warmth that words can't say.
A moment caught in fleeting light,
In this dance, the world gives way.

Through laughter shared and stories spun,
We weave our fates, a vibrant thread.
In every smile, a journey's begun,
In connection's glow, we are led.

Whispers travel on the breeze,
In the softest moments, hearts collide.
A flicker turns to fire with ease,
In vulnerability, we choose to bide.

So cherish these gentle sparks we share,
In every glance, let love unfold.
For in life's flickers, we find a prayer,
A connection crafted, a story told.

When Souls Speak

In deep silence, a truth unfolds,
When souls connect without a sound.
With eyes that shine and stories told,
In shared moments, we are unbound.

A glance reveals a thousand dreams,
Breaking barriers, crossing time.
In every sigh, a symphony gleams,
When two hearts meet, all is sublime.

Through the layers, we reach within,
Finding echoes of what we seek.
In the quiet, the magic begins,
When souls speak, words are weak.

Each heartbeat holds a universe,
In connection, life's mysteries blend.
Together, we craft our own verse,
Where beginnings and endings transcend.

So listen close when silence reigns,
For in these spaces, love ignites.
When souls speak freely, no one remains,
Outside the warmth of shared lights.

The Alchemy of Comfort

In the quiet of the night,
Whispers weave through the air,
Soft blankets hold the dreams tight,
Cradled in warmth, free from care.

A gentle touch holds the weight,
Of worries that fade to gray,
With each embrace, we appreciate,
The solace found in the stay.

Sipping tea with a friend near,
Laughter dances, spirits lift,
In shared moments, joy appears,
The heart's most precious gift.

Together we find our place,
In the glow of candlelight,
Every smile, a warm embrace,
Shining through the darkest night.

Alchemy in simple things,
Turn the mundane into gold,
In the comfort that love brings,
A story of warmth unfolds.

Radiant Ties

Beneath the stars, friendships grow,
Threads of laughter intertwine,
Hearts aligned in a gentle flow,
Through the years, they brightly shine.

Shared secrets and whispered dreams,
We build a fortress of trust,
In the silence, our spirit seems,
To flourish, it's simply a must.

Distance may try to divide,
But love knows neither time nor space,
In the heart, our bonds abide,
Radiant ties, impossible to erase.

Through storms and sunny days bright,
We stand together, side by side,
In every shadow and light,
Our connection is the true guide.

An unbreakable chain we forge,
With memories as our guide,
In every laugh, every surge,
Our radiant ties will forever abide.

A Mosaic of Feelings

Colors splash upon the canvas,
Each hue a story untold,
With every stroke, a new madness,
In the heart, warmth unfolds.

Fragments of laughter and tears,
Shattered pieces that combine,
In the gallery of our years,
Every moment, a divine sign.

Joy dances in vibrant red,
Sadness flows in deeper blue,
Hope is golden, gently spread,
As the mosaic comes into view.

Every shade, an experience,
Woven tightly, beautifully free,
In the fabric of existence,
A tapestry of what we see.

With each memory, we blend,
Crafting art from the mundane,
In the heart, love will mend,
Creating beauty from the pain.

Navigating the Unknown

On roads unseen, we take our flight,
Through shadows that whisper of fear,
With courage lighting the dark night,
We hold onto dreams that are dear.

Footsteps echo, uncertain but brave,
Charting paths where few have gone,
In the heart, a longing to save,
The essence of who we have drawn.

Waves crash while the compass spins,
Yet hope rises with each new dawn,
In this dance where chaos begins,
We find strength when all seems withdrawn.

The stars guide us through the haze,
Each twinkle a sign, a call,
In the wilderness, we blaze,
A journey that leads us through all.

With hands clasped, we brave the storm,
In unity, we conquer the night,
Through every shape, every form,
We navigate, hearts burning bright.

The Unseen Bond

In silence we linger, side by side,
A whisper of trust, where hearts collide.
Invisible threads weave through the air,
A bond formed in shadows, beyond compare.

Through storms we stand, unyielding and strong,
In laughter and tears, where we belong.
With every heartbeat, a rhythm so true,
In the tapestry woven, it's me and you.

Though miles may stretch, and voices may fade,
The warmth of connection will never evade.
In moments of doubt, remember the light,
The unseen bond shines, guiding us right.

In the quietest nights, when the world feels cold,
Our hearts are together, a story retold.
With each passing day, we gently embrace,
The unseen bond, our sacred space.

Hand in hand, through pathways unknown,
In the dance of our lives, we have grown.
A journey united, forever entwined,
In the essence of love, our souls aligned.

Steps in Shared Footprints

On golden sands, we carve our way,
With every step, we seize the day.
Footprints beside us, fading from view,
A testament of love, steadfast and true.

Through winding paths, beneath the stars,
Each journey shared, no matter how far.
In laughter and whispers, we find our voice,
In steps taken together, we make our choice.

In the dance of the seasons, we walk as one,
Through spring's tender blooms and summer's sun.
Each footprint a story, a memory's trace,
In shared embraces, we find our place.

As autumn leaves drift, and winter draws near,
We hold onto moments, cherish what's dear.
Through each change, each challenge, and test,
Steps in shared footprints, we find our rest.

Together we wander, through days unplanned,
In the journey of life, hand in hand.
Every footprint whispers, of where we've been,
In the dance of forever, it's you and me.

Colors of Care

In gentle strokes, we paint the sky,
With hues of compassion, a heartfelt sigh.
Vibrant and soft, like a warm embrace,
Colors of care, in every place.

From the smiles we share, to the tears we mend,
In the palette of life, love knows no end.
Each moment a brushstroke, a masterpiece true,
In colors of care, I find you anew.

The laughter of children, a bright sunny gold,
In moments of giving, our hearts unfold.
Through shades of support, we rise and we share,
An artist's creation, born from our care.

As twilight descends, painting the night,
We find in the darkness, a flicker of light.
In hues intertwined, our spirits embrace,
Colors of care, creating our space.

In life's rich canvas, together we stand,
Each color a bond, perfectly planned.
With every heartbeat, we bravely declare,
In the colors of care, we are always there.

Harmony in Heartbeats

In the stillness of night, a rhythm unfolds,
A song of our hearts, a story retold.
With every pulse, we dance in time,
Harmony flows, a seamless rhyme.

Through valleys of silence, and mountains of sound,
In each shared heartbeat, together we're found.
A melody whispered, soft and pure,
Harmony in heartbeats, forever endure.

As days turn to weeks, and seasons do shift,
In the cadence of love, we find our gift.
The harmony swells, like waves on the shore,
In the music of life, we crave for more.

In laughter and tears, our song intertwines,
A symphony sweet, with intricate lines.
With every heartbeat, the world feels so bright,
In harmony's embrace, we take flight.

So let us compose, with each passing day,
A duet of dreams, in every way.
In the rhythm of together, we boldly embark,
Harmony in heartbeats, a luminous spark.

Whispers of Kindred Spirits

In twilight's hush, we softly tread,
Each word like silk, where dreams are spread.
With laughter shared, and stories spun,
Two souls entwined, as one begun.

Through shadows cast, we find our way,
In gentle hearts, the light will play.
With every glance, a silent cheer,
As whispers dance, we draw you near.

Embracing truth, we rise and fall,
In quiet strength, we heed the call.
Together we weave, a tapestry bright,
For kindred spirits bask in light.

And like the stars that grace the night,
Our bond ignites, an endless flight.
With each heartbeat, we weave a song,
In harmony, where we belong.

So here we stand, through thick and thin,
With open hearts, let love begin.
For in this journey, side by side,
We'll light the path, our souls our guide.

The Silence Between Us

In quiet moments, words fall down,
A soft embrace, without a sound.
Yet in this stillness, feelings swell,
A whispered truth, we cannot tell.

Eyes meet in shadows, secrets shared,
A fragile trust, that must be bared.
In silence deep, our hearts align,
A bond unspoken, yet divine.

Emotions surge on this thin line,
Each heartbeat whispers, "You are mine."
In every pause, there lies the chance,
To understand, to learn, to dance.

Yet fear can grow where silence reigns,
A twisted path, of joy and pains.
But still we stand, through dark and bright,
With faith that grows, as day turns night.

So let us weave this woven thread,
Through silence shared, and paths we've tread.
In every quiet, our souls shall move,
A symphony that speaks of love.

Embracing Vulnerability

To shed the armor, let it fall,
In gentle light, we hear the call.
With open hearts, we take a chance,
In shared moments, we learn to dance.

In fragile truth, we find our might,
Through every tear, we reach for light.
No fear of shame, just tender grace,
In every heartbeat, we find our place.

In whispers soft, our stories blend,
With courage strong, we start to mend.
Each scar we wear, a badge of pride,
In this embrace, we won't divide.

As petals bloom in morning dew,
We blossom forth, we start anew.
With every breath, we claim our voice,
In vulnerability, we rejoice.

So step with me, take off the mask,
Together here, we'll face the task.
In trust we find, a brighter way,
Embracing all, come what may.

A Canvas of Understanding

On canvas wide, where dreams take flight,
With colors bright, we seek the light.
Each stroke a story, each hue a song,
Together we paint, where we belong.

With brushes dipped in hopes and fears,
We trace the paths through laughter, tears.
In vibrant shades, our spirits blend,
Creating worlds that never end.

Through texture rich, our truths unfold,
Sharing warmth against the cold.
With every layer, we learn to see,
In every mix, a symphony.

So let us paint with gentle hands,
Create a space where love expands.
With open minds, and hearts so wide,
Together here, we'll turn the tide.

And as the colors merge in time,
Our canvas speaks in perfect rhyme.
In this shared art, we can define,
A world of love, forever thine.

A Canvas of Compassion

In gentle strokes, we paint the day,
Colors blend in warm array.
With each kind deed, a brush we wield,
Creating hope, our hearts revealed.

Through empathy, our spirits grow,
In shadows cast, we let love flow.
A canvas bright, with stories shared,
In every heart, compassion dared.

Together, we weave a vibrant thread,
In every tear and joy we shed.
Each hue a moment, cherished bright,
A tapestry of shared delight.

With open hands, we shape our fate,
In every gesture, we cultivate.
The strokes of kindness, bold and free,
A masterpiece of unity.

As the world turns, let colors blend,
In every heart, let love transcend.
For in this canvas, we find our place,
In compassion's art, we embrace grace.

Harvesting Kindness

Beneath the sun, we sow the seeds,
Of gentle words and thoughtful deeds.
With each small act, the garden grows,
A bounty rich, the heart bestows.

In fields of care, we walk as one,
With every smile, a brighter sun.
We gather strength from those we share,
In kindness, we find love laid bare.

The fruits of labor, ripe and sweet,
In every heart, the love is meet.
Harvesting hope, we share our prize,
In gratefulness, our spirits rise.

So let us tend this sacred ground,
In every corner, kindness found.
Through giving hands, our hearts align,
In unity, our souls entwine.

As seasons change, let kindness bloom,
In every heart, dispelling gloom.
With every harvest, joy will share,
A garden rich, beyond compare.

The Dance of Shared Journeys

In every step, a tale unfolds,
As paths collide, and hands we hold.
With laughter bright, we share our song,
In every heart, we all belong.

Together we sway through joy and pain,
In every loss, in every gain.
The rhythm of life, a vibrant beat,
In shared journeys, we feel complete.

Through winding roads, we find our way,
In trust and hope, come what may.
Each twist and turn, a lesson learned,
In every heart, a fire burned.

With open minds, we'll greet the dawn,
Embracing change, as we go on.
In every dance, we weave our thread,
In unity, our fears are shed.

As stars align, our dreams take flight,
Together we soar, through day and night.
In every journey, hand in hand,
We write the story of our land.

Heartbeats in Resonance

In quiet moments, hearts align,
A rhythm soft, a sweet design.
Through whispered dreams, we find our sound,
In shared silence, love is found.

Each heartbeat echoes through the air,
A message clear, we truly care.
With every pulse, a bond we weave,
In harmony, we freely believe.

The dance of life, a sacred beat,
In every touch, our souls repeat.
Through trials faced, we stand as one,
In every storm, our love is spun.

As laughter rings, and tears may fall,
In every heart, we hear the call.
Together we sing, a timeless song,
In this resonance, we all belong.

So let the music play within,
In every heart, where love begins.
With every heartbeat, we shall rise,
In unity, beneath the skies.

Beneath Barriers

Whispers creep through heavy walls,
Silent echoes, distant calls.
Hearts encased in steel and stone,
Yearning for a place called home.

Hidden dreams in shadows lie,
Glimmers of a boundless sky.
With each crack, a spark of light,
Filling voids of endless night.

Time stands still, yet flows like streams,
Woven tightly in our dreams.
With strength, we push against the tide,
For freedom waits on the other side.

Barriers may try to confine,
But love can break each twisted line.
So we stand, and so we fight,
Chasing hopes that guide our flight.

Beneath the weight of stone and fear,
United souls can still draw near.
In the cracks where sunlight falls,
Together we will heed the calls.

Threads of Intent

Woven strands of golden hue,
Connecting hearts, both old and new.
With careful hands, we stitch our fate,
In every moment, we create.

A fragile web that holds us tight,
Through darkest days and brightest light.
Each intention, a gentle pull,
Binding dreams both rich and full.

Life's tapestry, with colors bright,
Dances softly, day and night.
In every thread, a story told,
Of hope, of love, as we grow old.

With every knot, a promise made,
In woven whispers, fears will fade.
Together we can break the mold,
With threads of intent, we are bold.

As we navigate this intricate design,
Embracing paths that intertwine.
We harness strength in unity,
For every thread is part of me.

In the Gaze of Strangers

In crowded streets, our eyes collide,
Fleeting moments, souls abide.
A glance can spark a hidden thrill,
Connect two hearts against their will.

A gentle smile, a brush of hands,
In silence shared, understanding stands.
Conversations without a sound,
In the gaze, true feelings found.

Strangers drift like clouds on high,
Yet in their presence, dreams can fly.
The world fades, and we become
Two souls entwined, lost in the hum.

In every stare, a story waits,
A universe behind the gates.
For in the glance, we often see,
The mirror of our own decree.

Though paths may part, and lives diverge,
In brief encounters, feelings surge.
Forever changed by what we found,
In the gaze of strangers, love surrounds.

Soft Encounters

Morning light through petals drapes,
A gentle touch that nature shapes.
In quiet corners, hearts entwine,
In soft encounters, love's design.

Breezes whisper on the skin,
Inviting warmth to flow within.
With every glance, the world stands still,
As moments bloom, our spirits thrill.

In laughter shared and stories spun,
The woven threads of two become one.
Soft encounters, sweet and kind,
In every heartbeat, love we find.

Through quiet times and gentle days,
We navigate life's winding ways.
In simple acts, a bond we weave,
In soft encounters, we believe.

As twilight falls, the stars ignite,
We cherish all we hold so tight.
In every whisper, every sound,
Soft encounters, love profound.

Echoes of Understanding

In silence we converse, thoughts set free,
Wisdom in whispers, a soft decree.
Hearts not just beating, but in tune,
A shared rhythm beneath the moon.

Eyes speak volumes, no words needed,
Empathy blooms where hope is seeded.
Gentle nods, a knowing glance,
In this vast world, we dance our chance.

Every smile holds a story told,
Every tear, a memory bold.
Together we rise, together we fall,
In laughter's embrace, we find it all.

Bridges built from moments shared,
Understanding grows, patiently bared.
In the echoes of voices, we hear
The universal language, crystal clear.

So let us hold this bond divine,
In shadows cast, our hearts align.
Merging paths, we pave the way,
In echoes, forever we'll sway.

Threads of Connection

With every heartbeat, threads intertwine,
Woven in stories, yours and mine.
Tales of joy, tales of strife,
In every stitch, a vibrant life.

Fingers trace paths of the past,
Moments captured, meant to last.
Each yarn a memory, brightly spun,
In the tapestry of two, we're one.

Through the fabric, warmth will flow,
Binding us close, helping us grow.
In the chaos, we find our peace,
A shared embrace that will never cease.

In laughter's echo, in sorrow's call,
Together we rise, together we fall.
Threads of connection, strong and true,
In every color, I see you.

A quilt of moments, stitched with care,
Feelings shared, burdens bare.
In the loom of life, we design,
A masterpiece, forever entwined.

Beneath Another's Skin

Beneath another's skin, we seek to know,
The depths of feelings, the truths that glow.
Every heartbeat, each pulse and sigh,
In shared vulnerability, we learn to fly.

Peeling layers, gentle and slow,
Unraveling fears as we brightly show.
In the mirror of eyes, we find our grace,
In this tender space, no need to race.

Words unsaid float in the air,
In the silence, we choose to share.
Stories hidden, like treasures glint,
In shared softness, we find the hint.

Wrapped in stories of each other's pain,
Through storms and shadows, hope will reign.
In the depths of connection, we start to mend,
Beneath another's skin, we transcend.

The warmth of hands, the gentlest touch,
In every heartbeat, it matters so much.
Together we tread on this delicate path,
Finding solace in love's quiet aftermath.

Shadows of Shared Stories

In shadows cast, our stories weave,
Tales of light, and dark reprieve.
With every laugh, a flicker ignites,
In the depths of night, our truth invites.

Silent whispers float through the air,
Echoes of lives we've chosen to share.
From heart to heart, the shadows blend,
A tapestry of moments that never end.

Through stormy days and sunlit streams,
Our laughter dances, intertwining dreams.
Each story spoken, a thread we tie,
In this vast expanse, we learn to fly.

In the hush of twilight, memories bloom,
Filling the void, dispelling gloom.
In shadows deep, our spirits soar,
Unveiling stories, forevermore.

Let the pages turn, let the chapters unfold,
In shadows of stories, love is bold.
Together we craft a legacy bright,
In the warmth of connection, we find our light.

The Dance of Compassion

In shadows where kindness gleams,
Hearts unite in gentle streams.
Whispers share the burdens deep,
In the dance, our spirits leap.

Hands extended, warmth enfolds,
Every story quietly told.
Weaving love in every glance,
Together, we find our chance.

Through pain and joy, we find our way,
In this bond, we choose to stay.
Compassion's light, a guiding star,
No matter how near or far.

Moonlight kisses faces bright,
In the dark we shine our light.
With every step, we grow as one,
In this dance, we're never done.

So let your heart embrace the flow,
In compassion's warmth, we grow.
Together we weave, together we thrive,
In this dance, we come alive.

Lives Interwoven

Threads of fate in colors blend,
Stories shared, as time we spend.
Woven patterns, rich and rare,
In each heartbeat, love laid bare.

From laughter's bloom to sorrow's thread,
Every moment where we've tread.
In the tapestry of dreams,
Life is brighter than it seems.

Hands and hearts create the seam,
Binding lives in a shared dream.
Every tear and every smile,
Makes the journey worth the while.

In quiet moments, bonds unwind,
A gentle touch, the ties that bind.
Through storms and sunny skies we weave,
In this fabric, we believe.

So cherish each connection true,
In this life, my heart is you.
Every life we touch and hold,
Interwoven, bright and bold.

The Silent Choir

In whispers soft, their voices rise,
A symphony beneath the skies.
With every note, hearts intertwine,
In silence, their hopes align.

Echoes of dreams in shades of light,
Through the dark, they bring delight.
In moments lost, they find the tune,
Guided by the silver moon.

Harmony, a gentle call,
Each breath shared, we stand tall.
Bound by thoughts that intertwine,
In this choir, we all shine.

The unspoken, a treasured bond,
In silence, we learn to respond.
Voices lifted, spirits soar,
In the quiet, we seek more.

So let the silent notes resound,
In every heart, a love profound.
Together in this sacred space,
The silent choir, an endless grace.

In the Valley of Understanding

In the valley where we stand,
Bridges built by gentle hands.
With every word, a seed we sow,
In the soil of love, let it grow.

Listening hearts, a place to share,
In this space, we show we care.
Empathy, our guiding light,
In the valley, wrong feels right.

Differences fade, like mist at dawn,
In the warmth, old wounds are gone.
Through dialogue, our souls align,
In understanding, we define.

So let us wander, hand in hand,
Through the valley, together we stand.
With open hearts, we freely roam,
In understanding, we find our home.

Cradled in Connection

In silent grace we gather close,
Our hearts entwined, a gentle dose.
Words like whispers, soft and kind,
A tapestry of souls aligned.

Through shared laughter, burdens fade,
In welcoming arms, our fears invade.
A bond that forms when shadows fall,
In unity, we stand so tall.

Each glance exchanged, a story spun,
Together we'll rise, two become one.
In every moment, rich and bright,
Our spirits soar, a shared light.

With every challenge that we face,
We find our strength in this warm space.
Embracing differences with grace,
Love's tender touch, our saving place.

Cradled in connection, we discover,
The essence of each loving other.
Together we weave, a life so true,
In this embrace, we start anew.

Vessels of Understanding

In the ocean vast, we sail and roam,
Each vessel crafted, a heart, a home.
Through storms we navigate, side by side,
With open minds, we turn the tide.

Listen closely to the tales we share,
Through every struggle, we find the air.
In quiet moments, wisdom flows,
A river deep where true love grows.

No distance great can break our bond,
With empathy's light, we journey fond.
We anchor deep in kindness shown,
In every heart, a place we've grown.

Through tangled paths, we seek the sun,
As vessels launched, our course begun.
Understanding blooms like flowers bright,
In every heart, we share the light.

Together we stand, hand in hand,
As vessels of hope in this vast land.
In every whisper, sincerity's sound,
We find our way—this love profound.

Lighthouses of Hope

When darkness falls, and waves crash high,
The lighthouses of hope flicker in the sky.
Guiding us through the tempest's grip,
With steadfast beams, we find our ship.

In the night's embrace, we raise our gaze,
To shining lights that set ablaze.
They whisper strength, they promise dawn,
In every beam, we carry on.

Through rocky shores and trials steep,
The lighthouses stand, their vigil keep.
In gentle tones, they call us home,
To shores of peace where hearts can roam.

In stormy seas, we find our way,
With every ray, we seize the day.
United, we break through the night,
As lighthouses of hope, we shine bright.

Together we stand, unwavering, bold,
In stories of courage, our fate unfolds.
In every heart, a lighthouse glows,
Leading us where the warm wind blows.

Navigating Common Waters

On gentle streams where currents blend,
We navigate, together as friends.
With sails unfurled, we chart the course,
In harmony, we find our force.

The waters calm, the ripples play,
In every twist, we learn the way.
Through valleys deep, and mountains high,
Together, we reach for the sky.

In shared endeavors, we grow anew,
Finding strength in the heart so true.
Each conversation, a paddle stroke,
In bonds of trust, our spirits woke.

With every challenge, hand in hand,
We carve our path through this vast land.
In common waters, our dreams unite,
Together we flourish, hearts in flight.

Like rivers flowing, side by side,
In every moment, warm and wide.
Navigating together, the journey's sweet,
In common waters, our souls complete.

Heartbeats in Sync

In the quiet night sky, stars alight,
Two souls drift gently, hearts in flight.
With every whisper, a bond is spun,
In the dance of silence, we are one.

The rhythm of laughter, shared and bright,
A melody flowing, pure delight.
Together we wander, hand in hand,
Among the echoes, we understand.

Time melts away, like snow in spring,
In each heartbeat, the joys we bring.
Life's tender moments, woven with care,
In this heartbeat's song, love fills the air.

Through storms that rage and shadows cast,
We chase the dawn, leaving doubts in the past.
For in this journey, our spirits bind,
Two hearts, one rhythm, endlessly aligned.

And as the sun sets, painting the sky,
Together we breathe, as dreams fly high.
With each pulse, our connection strengthens anew,
In the symphony of life, it's just me and you.

The Pulse of Humanity

In crowded streets where voices blend,
A tapestry of stories, hearts transcend.
Each face a tale of joy and strife,
We share the journey, the pulse of life.

With tears and laughter, we intertwine,
In the dance of struggle, hopes align.
Every heartbeat echoing a tune,
Underneath the sun, beneath the moon.

The whispers of kindness, soft and true,
Reminding us all of what we can do.
In every corner, a spark ignites,
Fueling the fire that guides our nights.

Within our unity, strength is found,
A global heartbeat, a sacred sound.
With outstretched hands, we pave the way,
For a brighter tomorrow, we'll not delay.

And as we gather, diverse and bold,
In the heart of humanity, stories unfold.
Together we rise, the anthem we sing,
In harmony's embrace, our spirits take wing.

An Embrace of Perspectives

In the realm of thoughts, where minds collide,
A tapestry woven, with colors wide.
Each viewpoint a brushstroke, bold and bright,
Creating a masterpiece, a shared insight.

Through lenses diverse, we learn to see,
The beauty in difference, unity's key.
In conversations whispered, debates that flare,
An embrace of perspectives, a world we share.

From valleys deep to mountains tall,
Every voice matters, we hear the call.
In the garden of ideas, seeds we plant,
Nurtured with care, together we chant.

With open hearts, we journey as one,
Chasing horizons, embracing the sun.
In this dance of dialogue, we find our place,
A mosaic of thoughts in a warm embrace.

So let us celebrate, share and grow,
In the vibrant spectrum, let compassion flow.
For in understanding, we find the grace,
An embrace of perspectives, our human space.

In the Cradle of Kindness

In the cradle of kindness, we find our rest,
A gentle cocoon, where hearts feel blessed.
With every gesture, a warmth bestowed,
In its tender light, love's burden is owed.

Like petals of flowers, soft and sweet,
Acts of compassion create a heartbeat.
A smile unspoken, a helping hand,
In the cradle of kindness, we all stand.

Through trials and tears, we lift each other,
A bond unbroken, sister and brother.
In shared laughter, or in silence deep,
In the cradle of kindness, our dreams we keep.

As seasons turn and moments fade,
Let's nurture the bonds that we have made.
For in this embrace, we learn to thrive,
In the cradle of kindness, love is alive.

So take a moment, let kindness flow,
In the garden of hearts, let compassion grow.
For in every act, life's beauty we find,
In the cradle of kindness, we are intertwined.

Oceans of Shared Experience

Waves of laughter rise and fall,
Carrying whispers, tales to tell.
In the depths, we find our call,
Navigating through this shell.

Tides of sorrow wash ashore,
Each moment shared, a gem, a spark.
Together we face every war,
Illuminating the dark.

Currents strong, but hearts align,
We drift, yet anchored side by side.
In this ocean, love will shine,
With every tide, our worlds collide.

Seas apart, but still so close,
Familiar shores in distant lands.
In every rise, a silent prose,
Through storms, we grasp each other's hands.

Through horizons vast and wide,
We sail with trust as our guide.
In these oceans, we abide,
Finding peace, where dreams collide.

Reflections from Within

In the mirror of my soul,
Echoes swirl, they twist and bend.
A quiet voice begins to toll,
A truth that yearns to transcend.

Shadows dance behind my eyes,
Flickers of doubt, whispers of dreams.
In the silence, hope still flies,
Woven deep within my seams.

Beneath the surface, waters stir,
Thoughts like currents ebb and flow.
Each reflection, a silent purr,
In stillness, I learn to grow.

Within the chaos, I will find,
The threads that bind both near and far.
Every struggle, thought entwined,
A tapestry, a guiding star.

From the depths, I rise anew,
A phoenix born from ashes deep.
In my heart, I know what's true,
As I embrace the dreams I keep.

The Space Where We Meet

In the silence where we pause,
A space where words become light.
Every heartbeat, every cause,
Draws us near, ignites the night.

Between the tension of desires,
Lies a moment, soft and vast.
We become like dancing fires,
Flames that flicker, shadows cast.

In this realm of trust we weave,
Hands extended, souls laid bare.
In our vulnerability,
The universe feels free to share.

With every glance, we pave the way,
A bridge built on tender grace.
In this space where hearts can play,
We find our own, our sacred place.

Time will bend, the world will shift,
Yet still we linger in this sphere.
Where peace, profound, becomes a gift,
In the meeting of our sphere.

Embracing Our Humanity

In the ebb and flow of life,
We stumble, rise, and learn to see.
Through joy and strife, as pure as knife,
We're weaving threads of unity.

With open hearts, we dare to share,
The broken parts, the mended seams.
In every moment, gentle care,
We find the strength within our dreams.

From every story, rich and diverse,
A quilt of voices, stitched with love.
In moments shared, we break the curse,
And rise together, hand in glove.

Though shadows linger, hope ignites,
We cultivate this fragile ground.
In every struggle, every fight,
Humanity is where we're found.

So let us gather, hand in hand,
Embracing all, both weak and strong.
In this soft and tender land,
We find our place, we all belong.

Hues of Humanity

In every shade, a story spins,
From dark to light, where life begins.
The brush of hands, the heart's own beat,
In vibrant tones, our souls compete.

To weave a tale of joy and tears,
A palette bright, through hopes and fears.
From deep cerulean to golden ray,
In every hue, we find our way.

The crimson love, the emerald grace,
In colors bold, we find our place.
With every glance, we're intertwined,
The hues of us, a love defined.

In every child, a vivid spark,
In colors rich, we leave a mark.
Together we paint this grand design,
In hues of love, our hearts align.

The Silent Embrace

In quiet rooms, where whispers dwell,
Two souls unite, a tale to tell.
With simple touch, emotions bloom,
A silent warmth dispels the gloom.

The world outside, a distant song,
In stillness found, where we belong.
Our hearts converse without a sound,
In silence, deeper love is found.

Amidst the noise, we seek the peace,
A gentle pause, a sweet release.
As time slips by, we hold it tight,
In quiet moments, pure delight.

Two hearts entwined, a quiet dance,
In hushed embrace, we find our chance.
No need for words, just you and me,
In silent love, we are set free.

Dancing in Another's Light

In shadows cast by others' grace,
We find our joy in their embrace.
With every step, a spark ignites,
In rhythms shared, our heart takes flight.

A gentle sway, a twirl, a glide,
In borrowed beams, we dare to hide.
Each laugh and sigh, a fleeting chance,
In shared delight, we learn to dance.

The glow of dreams, reflected bright,
Guides us through the longest night.
We twine our lives in borrowed beams,
In every glance, we trace our dreams.

Together lost in cosmic fate,
Our souls entwined, we resonate.
In luminous paths where hearts take flight,
We are alive, dancing in light.

In the Shoes of Strangers

Walk with me in another's stride,
Feel the weight they cannot hide.
Each step a tale, a life unknown,
In shoes of strangers, seeds are sown.

The burdens carried, unseen weight,
In quiet paths, we navigate.
To understand, we pause, we bend,
In every heart, we find a friend.

The stories shared, the laughter bright,
In every soul, a spark of light.
Through different lives, we start to see,
In every heart, a harmony.

So lace them up, the shoes we wear,
For empathy blooms when we dare.
In every journey, both near and far,
We find our truth, we find who we are.

Harmonies of Shared Pain

In shadows deep we find our way,
Hearts entwined in silent sway.
Each scar a note in sorrow's song,
Together here, where we belong.

Through whispered cries we share the load,
An echo of the pain we've sowed.
Yet in the ache, a bond we share,
Turning grief to love, we dare.

With every tear a truth unveiled,
In unity, our spirits sailed.
We bridge the gaps with tender hearts,
In harmonies, our strength imparts.

Through sleepless nights and weary days,
A melody of hope still plays.
From darkest depths, a light will rise,
In shared strife, we crystallize.

With gentle hands, we hold the pain,
Together we'll dance in the rain.
In the silence that softly reigns,
We find our peace, our shared remains.

A Whispering Breeze of Kindness

A breeze that speaks of gentle care,
Soft whispers dance upon the air.
In fleeting moments, kindness grows,
Like petals drifting, sweetly flows.

With open hearts, we freely give,
In tiny acts, we learn to live.
A smile shared can light the way,
Transforming night into bright day.

Through every touch, a spark ignites,
Compassion brews in endless flights.
Each deed a note within the song,
In harmony, we all belong.

Where shadows linger, kindness glows,
A beacon bright when darkness grows.
In every sigh, in every plea,
We find the strength to simply be.

Let laughter rise like morning sun,
And in that joy, we are as one.
For love's embrace will never cease,
In whispering breezes, we find peace.

The Reflection of Love's Light

In crystal pools where echoes gleam,
Love's reflection flows like a dream.
Each glance a spark, each smile a ray,
Illuminating the darkest day.

From gentle words, the heart does swell,
A story told, a magic spell.
In laughter shared and moments pure,
We find a light that will endure.

Through trials faced, our spirits shine,
In love's embrace, our souls align.
A warmth that wraps, a safety found,
In tender bonds, forever bound.

When shadows creep and doubts arise,
In love's reflection, we become wise.
With every heartbeat, truth is sung,
In silent vows, our tale is spun.

Through every tear and every fight,
Love's radiant glow ignites the night.
In this embrace, our hopes take flight,
Together we shine, love's pure light.

The Rain of Understanding

In gentle drops, the truth descends,
A soothing drench that never ends.
With every splash, a story told,
In rain of understanding, we unfold.

It washes fears from weary minds,
In droplets soft, compassion binds.
Each moment shared, a bridge we build,
In stormy skies, our hearts are filled.

Through tempests fierce and winds that wail,
We find our strength when all seems frail.
With every storm, we learn to bend,
In rain of understanding, we mend.

The world may roar, but we hold fast,
In this embrace, the die is cast.
For in each drop, a lesson flows,
In empathy, our power grows.

So let it rain and cleanse our souls,
As kindness whispers, love consoles.
In every storm, together stand,
In rain of understanding, hand in hand.

Embracing Shadows

In twilight's hush, shadows dance,
Whispers of dreams beneath the trees.
Fear not the night, give it a chance,
For in the dark, we'll find our peace.

Beneath the stars, secrets unfold,
Hopes wrapped in the night's embrace.
With every sigh, stories retold,
In shadows' arms, we find our place.

The moonlight glows, a gentle guide,
Casting light on paths unknown.
Through worries bright, we must abide,
In every step, we're never alone.

Embrace the dusk, let worries fade,
In every shadow, find your way.
Through trials faced, a bond is made,
Together we'll brave the end of day.

So take my hand, where darkness lies,
We'll wander through the veils of night.
In every glance, the spirit flies,
Embracing shadows, finding light.

Tides of Compassion

The ocean breathes with gentle grace,
Waves kiss the shore, a soothing sound.
In tides of love, we find our place,
Understanding grows where hearts abound.

With every swell, a heartfelt plea,
Kindness flows like the endless sea.
Together we rise, a bond we see,
In tides of compassion, harmony.

When storms arise and skies turn gray,
We'll stand as one, unyielding, strong.
Through every tide, we'll find the way,
In one another, we all belong.

So let us share this timeless dance,
With open hearts and gentle hands.
In life's grand waves, we're given chance,
To lift each other as love expands.

As water ebbs, the truth revealed,
A world where warmth and care abide.
In tides of compassion, hearts are healed,
Together we'll flow, the rising tide.

Echoes of Kindness

Amidst the noise, a soft refrain,
Echoes of kindness drift through time.
A gentle touch can heal the pain,
With simple words, our souls can climb.

In every smile, a spark ignites,
A chain reaction, love defined.
Through darkest days and brightest nights,
The power of kindness is intertwined.

Let compassion ripple, like a stream,
A helping hand, a heart so pure.
Through every challenge, let us dream,
In echoes of kindness, we endure.

From mountain tops to valleys low,
Each act of love can change a life.
In tender moments, wisdom grows,
Through kindness shared, we overcome strife.

So let us sow these seeds of grace,
In every heart, a future bright.
With echoes of kindness, we'll embrace,
The beauty found within the light.

A Tapestry of Lives

Threads of stories, woven tight,
Intertwined in a vibrant weave.
Each life a color, bold and bright,
In this tapestry, love won't leave.

From laughter shared to tears we shed,
Each moment captured, a precious thread.
In this design, the heart can spread,
A tapestry of lives that we've led.

Through every challenge, through every fight,
The patterns twist and turn with grace.
In unity's glow, so warm and light,
Together we'll find our rightful place.

As seasons change and years unfold,
New patterns join the ones before.
With every story, a life retold,
In this rich tapestry, we soar.

So let us weave with heart and mind,
A legacy of love and strife.
In every stitch, a truth we'll find,
Together, we craft this tapestry of life.

The Dances of Life's Symphony

In the hall of fleeting dreams,
Each note weaves a story bright.
Twilight whispers, shadows gleam,
Life dances on in soft twilight.

With every step, our hearts align,
Melodies bind us, a gentle embrace.
In harmony, the stars intertwine,
Together we find our sacred space.

Through laughter shared, through pain we mend,
The symphony plays, forever anew.
In every rhythm, we comprehend,
Life's dance is our sacred cue.

With drums of hope and strings of dreams,
The world spins round, a vibrant sphere.
In every glance, a love redeems,
As life unfolds, our song is clear.

So let us sway on this grand stage,
In life's symphony, we all partake.
With every turn, we write a page,
Together in the music we make.

Treading the Path of Another

On winding roads where shadows play,
I tread softly upon your way.
With each step, we share the light,
In your journey, my heart takes flight.

Through valleys low and mountains high,
In silent whispers, we shall fly.
Your dreams unfurl, I hold them tight,
Together, we carve shadows bright.

With open hearts, our paths entwine,
In the silence, our souls align.
Every tear, each joy, we share,
In walking forth, we show we care.

You teach me grace, you show the way,
With every dawn, a brand-new day.
In moments lost, in time's embrace,
Treading paths, we find our place.

So hand in hand, let us proceed,
With every step, your heart I heed.
In every stride, our fates combine,
Together we shine, your dreams are mine.

The Pulse of Togetherness

In the quiet hum of night,
Our hearts pulse as one, so bright.
With every beat, a bond renews,
In togetherness, we find our cues.

Whispers shared beneath the stars,
In this dance, we cross the bars.
Every heartbeat tells a tale,
Of love's journey, we shall sail.

Steps in sync, we move as one,
Underneath the glowing sun.
With laughter bright, with tears so sweet,
Together, we craft our heartbeat.

In stormy weather, side by side,
With open arms, our fears we bide.
In every challenge, hand in hand,
The pulse of life, we understand.

So let us dance, let spirits rise,
In this union, love never dies.
With every thrum, our souls are blessed,
In the pulse of life, we find our rest.

A Tapestry of Togetherness

Threads of laughter, colors bright,
Woven tales in soft moonlight.
Each moment stitched, a precious glance,
In this tapestry, we dance.

With loving hands, we craft our fate,
Interwoven dreams we celebrate.
Every joy, each tear we share,
In togetherness, we learn to care.

Patterns bloom in unity's glow,
With every heartbeat, our love we sow.
In tangled threads, we find our way,
A beautiful mix, come what may.

Through storms we weather, brightly shine,
Each piece a story, yours and mine.
In every layer, a bond so true,
Together, this tapestry we construe.

So here's to us, the moments drawn,
In this fabric, our hearts are sewn.
In the weave of life, we shall stay,
A tapestry of love, come what may.

In the Footsteps of Others

We walk where shadows blend,
Tracing paths of those who went.
Echoes in the silent night,
Guiding us towards the light.

Their dreams whisper in the breeze,
Among the rustling of the trees.
Lessons carved in time's embrace,
We find our strength in their grace.

With every step, we honor past,
Learning from the shadows cast.
Together, we rise and fall,
In unity, we stand tall.

The footprints left upon the sand,
A story woven, hand in hand.
We journey forth, ever bold,
In the tapestry of lives retold.

So let us tread with care and love,
With guidance from the stars above.
In the footsteps of the meek,
Find the strength in what we seek.

Colors of Compassion

Paint the world with shades of care,
A brush of kindness everywhere.
With every stroke, a heart can heal,
In vibrant hues, our spirits feel.

A palette rich in love's embrace,
Each color tells a warm, sweet grace.
Blue for calm and green for growth,
Each hue reminds us, we are both.

Yellow shines like morning's light,
Bringing joy, chasing the night.
In every sigh, in every smile,
Find the spark to make life worthwhile.

Orange beats with passion's flame,
Fires of hope that never tame.
In every moment, every chance,
Colors dance in a vibrant prance.

Let compassion be our guiding brush,
In a world that often rush.
Together, we create the art,
A masterpiece from every heart.

Beneath the Surface

What lies beneath the still, calm tide?
Secrets and dreams, in silence, hide.
With every wave, a tale unfolds,
Of hearts untouched, of lives untold.

Dark waters hold the burdens deep,
Silent whispers that never sleep.
Beneath the calm, a tempest brews,
In depths of blue, the storm renews.

Each ripple tells a story fine,
Of love and loss, of hope's design.
Dive beneath and you will find,
The hidden gems of soul and mind.

In quiet thought, the currents flow,
An ocean vast, where feelings grow.
Beneath the surface, life persists,
In shadows cast, a world exists.

So take a plunge, let go of fear,
Explore the depths, the truth draws near.
Life's secrets hide within the blue,
Beneath the surface, finding you.

The Language of Heartbeats

In the rhythm of our hearts,
A silent song that never parts.
Each beat a word, each pause a sigh,
In the language we share, you and I.

Emotions flow in steady streams,
Carving paths through whispered dreams.
With every thump, a beat that speaks,
In love's embrace, the heart finds peaks.

Listen closely, can you hear?
The sweetest notes draw ever near.
In tenderness, our souls entwine,
Creating symphonies divine.

A heartbeat tells of joys and fears,
Of laughter shared, of uncried tears.
In this dance, we find our grace,
In each pulse, a warm embrace.

Let us speak in rhythms sweet,
With every heartbeat, our lives meet.
In the language of our shared fate,
Find solace in love, never wait.

A Symphony of Silences

In quiet spaces, whispers play,
Gentle notes that drift away.
Each pause a melody unwinds,
A heart's soft echo, still it finds.

Beneath the stars, a hush so bright,
The world retreats from day to night.
In silent realms, our dreams take flight,
A symphony of pure delight.

The secrets linger, veiled in grace,
In hurried breaths, we find our place.
In every silence, truths emerge,
A soundless song, our spirits surge.

With every heartbeat, silence reigns,
In unvoiced feelings, love remains.
In stillness, worlds collide and blend,
A symphony that knows no end.

Threads of Harmonious Hearts

We weave our dreams with gentle care,
In colors bright, beyond compare.
Each thread a bond, a tale to share,
Connected souls, through love we dare.

In laughter's glow, we stitch the night,
With every smile, our hopes take flight.
A tapestry of pure delight,
In harmony, our hearts unite.

Through trials faced, our fabric weaves,
In moments shared, our spirit believes.
Each knot a story, love achieves,
In every stitch, a heart receives.

Together dancing, side by side,
In rhythm's flow, our passions glide.
A song of joy, our hearts abide,
In threads of love, we take our ride.

The Footprints We Leave

In sandy shores or paths we tread,
Each step a story, softly said.
The footprints linger, fade away,
In memories of yesterday.

Through fields of time, we walk along,
Each trace a note in life's own song.
In shadowed light, where dreams belong,
The footprints tell where we are strong.

With every journey, lessons learned,
The bridges crossed, the fires burned.
Each footprint echoes, softly yearned,
In every heart, a flame returned.

Though paths may vanish in the night,
The essence lingers, pure and bright.
In every step, a chance for flight,
The footprints guide us to the light.

Beneath the Common Sky

Under the vast and starry dome,
We find our place, we make our home.
In every glance, a universe,
Connected souls in silence converse.

Through clouds that drift and raindrops fall,
We stand together, one and all.
In nature's breath, we hear the call,
Beneath this sky, we rise, we crawl.

In every sunset, colors blend,
In every dawn, a chance to mend.
Together, hearts and hands extend,
In this shared space, we all transcend.

Beneath the sky, with dreams afire,
In unity, we lift higher.
A tapestry of hearts inspired,
Together we weave our one desire.

Cracks and Crevices of Care

In the quiet nooks we find,
Tender thoughts lost to time.
Through the fissures love will seep,
In the shadows, hearts will climb.

Each small gesture softly glows,
Bridges built on fragile bows.
Even in the toughest stone,
A gentle touch can find a home.

Whispers cradle weary nights,
Healing souls with whispered lights.
Even cracks can hold a tale,
Of strength that never seems to pale.

Life's embrace in every crack,
Nurtured bonds won't fade or lack.
In the crevices, we learn,
To cherish all for which we yearn.

So let us treasure what we find,
In hidden spaces, intertwined.
For cracks and crevices declare,
That love exists in every layer.

Flickers of Light in Darkness

In the night when shadows creep,
A spark of hope begins to leap.
Glimmers soft and faintly glow,
Guiding souls through depths of woe.

Moments shared beneath the stars,
Finding solace, healing scars.
Even when the world feels cold,
Flickers of warmth begin to mold.

In the silence, whispers grow,
Tales of courage gently flow.
Through the dark, we hold on tight,
To each flicker, chasing light.

Bonds ignited by those beams,
Chasing away our hidden dreams.
Together, we will find our way,
As flickers turn to brighter day.

So lift your eyes and see the signs,
Each flicker sparks a world that shines.
In unity, our spirits soar,
Through darkness, we can find the door.

Silent Bonds

In the space where words don't tread,
Connection blooms, an unseen thread.
In the quiet, hearts align,
Silent promises intertwine.

Through the laughter and the tears,
Understanding calms our fears.
No need for grand displays of might,
In stillness, love ignites the night.

Shared glances speak a thousand tales,
Whispered thoughts like gentle gales.
Even when the world is loud,
Together, we stand unbowed.

In the silence, we find grace,
Every heartbeat, a warm embrace.
Resilient chords of friendship strong,
Breathe together, where we belong.

So let us cherish moments rare,
In silence, love's quiet flare.
For bonds unspoken hold us near,
In the stillness, we draw near.

The Rivulets of Reach

Through the valleys, rivers flow,
Carving paths, gently, slow.
Each rivulet, a tale untold,
Of journeys new and feelings bold.

In the currents, life's embrace,
Dancing droplets, leaving trace.
As fingers touch the water's gleam,
We find ourselves within the stream.

Reaching out, we learn to give,
In the flow, we truly live.
With open hearts, we bridge the seams,
Building futures from our dreams.

Every bend has stories spun,
Of battles fought, of races run.
Together as we drift and sway,
In rivulets, we find our way.

So cherish every gentle move,
For in each curve, our souls improve.
The rivulets of reach will teach,
The beauty lies in love's sweet breach.

Silent Conversations

In the stillness, words unsaid,
Eyes meet softly, hearts unfed.
Whispers dance in the evening air,
Silence speaks of love laid bare.

Fingers trace the outline of dreams,
Unraveled stories, so it seems.
A gaze that lingers, warmth concealed,
In quiet moments, truths revealed.

Shadows flicker in the twilight glow,
Silent echoes of what we know.
Unspoken bonds that grow with time,
In this hush, our spirits climb.

The world outside fades to a blur,
Within this space, just you and her.
Time unwinds with each breath shared,
A tapestry of realms declared.

In gentle pauses, life unfolds,
The warmth of presence, love enfolds.
A world of thoughts weaves in the night,
In silent conversations, pure delight.

In the Touch of a Hand

Fingertips brush like feathered dreams,
In a moment's pause, the world redeems.
The warmth of skin, electricity,
In the touch of a hand, we feel free.

Holding tight through the stormy mayhem,
A gentle squeeze, as hearts awaken.
In this small gesture, safe and sound,
A universe of feelings found.

Each heartbeat syncs, a silent song,
In this connection, we belong.
Laughter dances at fingertips' play,
In the touch of a hand, joys sway.

A crush of palms, a steady pulse,
In simple gestures, love convulse.
Beyond all words, a truth so grand,
Life unfolds in the touch of a hand.

Together, we build castles in air,
Each embrace shows how much we care.
In every moment, love withstands,
In the beauty found in gentle hands.

Fragments of Shared Journeys

We wander paths both worn and new,
Each step a piece of me and you.
With every story, our hearts entwine,
In fragments of journeys that brightly shine.

Laughter echoes through sunlit days,
In memories made, we'll always stay.
Every bump and turn builds our lore,
Adventure awaits behind each door.

Winding roads that twist and turn,
Lessons learned from fires that burn.
In the tapestry of time and space,
Fragments weave our sacred place.

Silent nights bring whispered dreams,
In shared journeys, freedom beams.
Holding hands as the stars align,
Under the moon, our spirits shine.

Tomorrow calls with promises bright,
With open hearts, we chase the light.
In the fabric of time, we will find,
Fragments of journeys, soulfully aligned.

Empathy's Quiet Song

In the stillness, hearts converse,
With soft whispers, we immerse.
A gentle nod, a knowing glance,
In empathy's song, we take a chance.

Streams of feelings flowing free,
In shared silence, you and me.
Echoes of hurt, a bond we share,
In vulnerability, we lay bare.

With every sigh, a truth unfurls,
In quiet shadows, compassion swirls.
We listen close, attuned to pain,
In empathy's song, hope remains.

United in this shared refrain,
A melody that eases strain.
Holding space with open hearts,
In whispered tunes, healing starts.

Together we rise, through dark and light,
In harmony, we'll find our flight.
Let kindness be our guiding throng,
In the beauty of empathy's song.

When Hearts Align

In twilight's glow, two souls take flight,
Stars whisper softly, igniting the night.
Dreams intertwine, like vines that embrace,
In the dance of love, we find our place.

Moments like raindrops, they shimmer and fall,
Echoes of laughter, the sweetest call.
Time stands still, as we lose our way,
In a world woven with threads of the day.

Eclipsed by the shadows, we shine so bright,
Guided by hope, we reach for the light.
With every heartbeat, two rhythms blend,
Life's gentle song, a tale without end.

Hand in hand, through the storms we tread,
Facing the future, never misled.
When hearts align, the journey is free,
In each other's eyes, we learn to see.

Together we wander, no need for a map,
Each moment a treasure, each hug a wrap.
In the silence waiting, a promise we'll find,
In love's endless echo, two hearts entwined.

Voices of the Unheard

Echoes of silence fill the vast air,
Lost are the stories, binding despair.
In crowded rooms, they quietly stand,
Voices like whispers, slipping through sand.

Eyes tell the secrets, words cannot share,
Truth in their silence often laid bare.
Seeking connection, yet feeling alone,
In the midst of a crowd, they wander unknown.

Hearts carry burdens, heavy and raw,
Yearning for someone to pause and draw.
In kindness and courage, let's break the chains,
Listen to souls, feel their pains.

Beneath the surface, life's stories unfold,
In every quiet heart, tales yet untold.
What if compassion became the new way?
We'd paint a new world, where hope starts to sway.

Let us unite, lend an ear to the shy,
In the chorus of life, their dreams learn to fly.
Together we'll rise, lighting pathways anew,
Voices of the unheard, worthy of view.

Garden of Shared Feelings

In the garden of shared feelings, we bloom,
Petals of trust, dispel the gloom.
Roots intertwine, beneath the ground,
Nurtured by kindness, where love can be found.

Each blossom tells tales, vibrant and bright,
Whispers of dreams, dancing in light.
In the shade of the trees, we pause and reflect,
Finding the pathways that life can connect.

Fragrance of memories, sweet on the air,
Together we flourish, beyond every care.
Seasons of laughter, of joy and of tears,
Side by side, we conquer our fears.

Together we tend to this sanctuary,
Where hearts share their stories, a soliloquy.
With every embrace, the colors ignite,
In this garden of feelings, we find our delight.

As petals fall softly, in a gentle array,
We cherish the moments, come what may.
In the garden of life, love grows ever strong,
Nurtured with patience, where all can belong.

The Weight of a Kind Word

An act of grace, a gentle touch,
The weight of a kind word, it can mean so much.
In a world that often feels harsh and cold,
A single sweet whisper can turn hearts to gold.

Lifted by kindness, a spirit can soar,
Creating connections that open a door.
With empathy's light, we mend and align,
In the tapestry of life, your heart and mine.

When shadows loom close, and doubts start to creep,
A kind word can cradle, help silence the weep.
Each syllable spoken, a seed softly sown,
That grows into hope, through the love that we've grown.

In the clamor of life, let our voices resound,
With messages tender, let love know no bound.
For healing is powerful, a beacon of grace,
A kind word directed can lighten the space.

So speak from the heart, let your truth freely flow,
In a world needing kindness, your light can bestow.
With every exchange, let compassion unfurl,
Together we flourish, making magic in this world.

Navigating Invisible Currents

Beneath the surface, whispers flow,
Secrets mingling with the undertow.
Lost in tides, we drift and sway,
Searching for the light of day.

In shadows deep, emotions dance,
Caught in ripples of chance romance.
With every pull, we learn to steer,
Through murky waters, moving near.

Garlands made of dreams unspoken,
Threads of hope, yet never broken.
We ride the waves of joy and pain,
Navigating through love's terrain.

Each wave a lesson, each swell a guide,
In currents strong, we must decide.
To trust the flow or fight the stream,
In silent waters, we find our dream.

Together we sail, hand in hand,
Through the chaos, we make our stand.
With hearts aligned and spirits free,
In invisible currents, you and me.

Tuning Forks of the Heart

In softest whispers, feelings chime,
Resonance found in moments sublime.
Every heartbeat sings a song,
Tuning forks where we belong.

Like echoes in a quiet room,
Our love ignites, dispelling gloom.
Harmonies thrill, a sweet embrace,
Two souls united in timeless space.

With every laugh, a note rings clear,
Melodies crafted from joy and fear.
Life's symphony we boldly play,
Tuning forks guide us on our way.

In the cadence of our tender ties,
Every glance a world of sighs.
Together we dance, both near and far,
In the music of life, you are my star.

Let us compose this journey's score,
With rhythms deep, forevermore.
In perfect pitch, we find our part,
As tuning forks awaken the heart.

In the Garden of Feelings

In the garden where roses bloom,
Love's soft fragrance fills the room.
Petals whisper secrets of time,
Roots entwined, a dance sublime.

Sunlight trickles through the leaves,
As laughter weaves through all it cleaves.
Joy and sorrow intertwine so,
In this garden, we learn to grow.

With every step, a memory sown,
In fertile soil, our hearts have grown.
Together we cultivate the light,
In the garden of feelings, day and night.

Ivy climbs on walls of trust,
Through trials, we bloom from dust.
Side by side, we tend and mend,
In this sanctuary, love won't end.

Seasons change, but still we stand,
In the garden, hand in hand.
Through blooms of hope and shades of pain,
Our love flourishes, forever the same.

Unfolding Hearts

In gentle folds, our stories lie,
Like paper cranes that learn to fly.
Each crease a memory we hold,
In unfolding hearts, our truths unfold.

With every breath, we learn to trust,
Through tender moments, love is a must.
In whispers shared, a secret art,
Together we mend what time may part.

Dancing shadows in twilight's glow,
Our hearts reveal what we both know.
In delicate patterns, we intertwine,
As petals open, your heart in mine.

Unfolding slowly, a beautiful pace,
Layer by layer, we dare to embrace.
With every heartbeat, a new refrain,
In the tapestry of love, joy and pain.

So let us weave this tale divine,
In the fabric of dreams, our hearts align.
Through every chapter, we will find,
In unfolding hearts, our souls entwined.

Layers of Laughter and Tears

In the dance of joy, we play,
Gleaming smiles on a bright day.
Yet beneath the vibrant hue,
Soft whispers of sorrow too.

Laughter's echo fills the air,
Moments spun with tender care.
Tears that glisten, hearts that mend,
A cycle that will never end.

Through the trials we often meet,
We find strength in love's heartbeat.
Every layer tells a tale,
Of brighter paths and darker trails.

In laughter's glow, the shadows hide,
Hope and grief walk side by side.
With every tear, a lesson learned,
In joy and pain, our hearts have turned.

So let us weave both threads with grace,
Embrace the smiles, the fears we face.
For in this dance of light and shade,
Life's tapestry is brightly laid.

The Fabric of Connection

Stitched together by a thread,
In quiet moments, bonds are fed.
Hands reach out to seek the light,
In the darkness, we unite.

Voices blend in harmony,
Sharing dreams, a symphony.
With every word, a bridge is built,
In love's embrace, we shed our guilt.

Moments linger, memories grow,
Through laughter's kiss and sorrow's flow.
Connection blooms like flowers bright,
Guiding us through day and night.

In silence shared, we find the dawn,
Two souls entwined, forever drawn.
The fabric woven, strong and true,
In every thread, a part of you.

So wrap me in your gentle care,
In this fabric, we both share.
Together we shall stand so tall,
With love's embrace, we conquer all.

Ebb and Flow of Heartfelt Moments

The tide of time comes in and out,
Waves of warmth mingled with doubt.
Moments cherished, fleeting fast,
Embrace the now, forget the past.

In gentle whispers, secrets told,
Hearts like treasures, brimming gold.
Each heartbeat swells, a rising tide,
In ebb and flow, our dreams abide.

Through sunlit days and stormy nights,
We navigate with hopeful sights.
Love's pulse keeps us in the dance,
In the rhythm, we take our chance.

Hold me close when shadows loom,
In the quiet, we find room.
To breathe together, hearts in sync,
In every moment, love's sweet link.

So ride the waves, let currents guide,
Through every rush and gentle tide.
In this flow, we're never lost,
For in each moment, love's the cost.

Shadows of Suffering and Joy

In the stillness, shadows creep,
Where memories and sorrows seep.
Yet from the dark, a light will spark,
In the depths, we find our heart.

Joy can flourish from the pain,
Like blooms that rise after the rain.
Each struggle is a thread we sew,
In life's quilt, both high and low.

Through the valleys of despair,
We seek the strength to truly care.
For in suffering, we grow wise,
With every tear, the spirit flies.

Hold my hand, let's face the night,
In darkness, we will find the light.
Together through the storm we roam,
In each shadow, we find home.

So let our laughter break the gloom,
And let love's warmth fill every room.
In the dance of joy and strife,
Together we embrace our life.

Milton Keynes UK
Ingram Content Group UK Ltd.
UKHW030751121124
451094UK00013B/768